THE BREXIT RHYMES

MIKE PEARCE

DEDICATION

This book is dedicated to all those who made Brexit
happen against all odds

GOD BLESS GREAT BRITAIN

CONTENTS

Acknowledgment
Preview

Happy Brexit song   1

Hands faces UKIP woes/This little deal went to market   3

Here we go round the Brexit fears   4

Bercow, Bercow pudding and pie   5

Britain's Hope so very close   6

Mrs May, Mrs May where have you been?/Mrs May   7
defroster what would it cost her?

Boris had a stumbling block   8

Restrictions and closures say the bells of remainers   9

Bah, Bah Boris have you any pull?/There was a little   10
deadlock

A showdown in the commons rang like a bell   11

Simple Simon met a tariff   12

Now Farage, Now May /Little Brussels parliament sat in 13
the corner

What are British fishermen made of   14

Old Mother Hubbard went to the cupboard   15

It had so many variants just like the flu   16

Oh the grand old Euro pact

Round and round the world trade/Two little trade deals sitting on the wall — 17

One potato, two potatoes/Cock a doodle doo/Solitary, solitary how does your garden grow — 18

Boris put the kettle on/ Diddle Diddle dumpling — 19

Ring a ring of customs/Three gunboats not nice — 20

The North wind doth blow/Interest rates are falling down — 21

Wee Willie lorries runs through the town — 22

Oh dear what can the matter be? — 23

One two, De Gaul blocks EU — 24

ACKNOWLEDGMENTS

The author would like to thank Christine Pearce
for reading and checking through the manuscript.

PREVIEW

In times of danger, stress or epidemics rhymes or songs were often made up as reminders of hazards that can affect us all. Withdrawal from the EU Brexit has taken many years like an eternal ping pong match and had reached a point where people were fed up with it. It has now happened at the eleventh hour just before Christmas 2020 opening a new era for Britain to try and make itself a bit greater than it was.

Here is a selection based on familiar nursery rhymes.

THE HAPPY BREXIT SONG

If you're happy and you know it
wave your flag
If you're happy and you know it
wave your flag
If you're happy and you know it
and you really want to show it
If you're happy and you know it
wave your flag

If you're happy and you know it
catch British fish
If you're happy and you know it

catch British fish

If you're happy and you know it

and you really want to show it

 If you're happy and you know it

catch more British fish

If you're happy and you know it

trade worldwide

If you're happy and you know it

trade worldwide

If you're happy and you know it

and you really want to show it

 If you're happy and you know it

trade world wide

Hands, faces, UKIP woes

Hands, spaces, UKIP woes

Don't say leave or violence to
Farage grows

Hands, faces, milkshake throws

This little deal went to market

This little deadlock stayed at home

This little speaker caused great grief

And this little Brexiteer caused
none

While this little PM cried, we're
French, wee, wee, and ran all the
way home

Here we go round the Brexit fears

The Brexit fears the Brexit fears

Here we go round the Brexit fears

with a Grieve and Bercow warning

This is the way we shout them

down, shut them down, shout them

down

This is the way we shout them

down (suspend parliament, take

back control, keep apart) on a cold

parliamentary morning

Bercow, Bercow pudding and pie

Was a remainer and doesn't know
why

When the peers go all away

Mr John Bercow will come out to
play

Britain's hope so very close; its
effect was quite a blow

As everywhere that Mrs. May went
the MPs always said no

Corbyn sabotaged her at school one
day

Which was against the rule

It made the soft deal stay away
which to some was super cool

Mrs May, Mrs. May where have you been?

been?

I've been to Brussels to negotiate a dream

Mrs. May Mrs. May what did you there?

I met a lot of EU saboteurs, it's just not fair!

May defroster what would it cost her

When the showdown came

She kept in a bubble

And got into trouble

And never went there again

Boris had a stumbling block

And France was hot and reckless

That's the way that deadlock goes

When you couldn't care less

Restrictions and closures say the
bells of remainers

You owe me concessions say the
bells of repressions

When will you grant me a deal says
the bells of 11th hour appeal?

When there's no glitch say the bells
of French itch

When will that be says the Boris for
sovereignty

I do not know says the bells of
sweet sorrow

Here comes a level playing field to
put you to bed

And here comes new Brexit to
chop off your head

Bah bah   Boris have you any pull

Yes sir, yes sir I've given them

some bull.

One for the Barnier and one for the

Tusk one for the

Macron who is also very brusque

There was a little deadlock and it

had a little spike

Which right at the time was so

torrid

When it was good it was very very

good

but when it was bad it was horrid

A showdown in the commons rang

like a bell

It invaded the public and made us

unwell

All the soft dealers and all no deal

men

Couldn't stop Brexit from

happening again

Simple Simon met a tariff going to

the fair

Said Simple Simon to the tariff

 Don't you dare come near.

Says the tariff to Simple Simon

Symptoms there are many

Says Simple Simon to the tariff

Thank God I don't have any

Now Farage now May, now
Barnier, Van der Leyen
On Corbin, Frost,
On Johnson and Gove all is not
lost
To the top of the world a country
so small
Now thrash away, thrash away,
thrash away all

Little Brussels parliament sat in the
corner eating his Christmas pie
He ceased to ask and started to
multitask
And said you're an isolated guy

What are British fishermen made
of?

 What are British fishermen made
of?

Catches and quotas and nets full of
bloaters

That's what British fishermen are
made of.

What are little businesses made of?

What are little businesses made of?

Profits and taxes when import
relaxes that's what little businesses
are made of

Old Mother Hubbard went to the
cupboard to get her poor dog a
bone
But when she got there the shelves
were bare
And so the poor dog had none

It had so many variants just like the
flu
They gave it some wrath
To solve it they said
And whipped up an agreement
To put it to bed

Oh the grand old Euro pact

They put a lockdown then

They marched us up to the top of

the hill

And marched us down again

When we were up we were up

And when we were down we were

down

and when we were only halfway up

He knocked us down again

Subsidies, subsidies go away

And don't come back some other

day

Round and round the world trade
that we all will share
One step two steps we'll export it
everywhere.

Two little trade deals sitting on the
wall
One named global, the other named
control
Bounce back economy, bounce
back jobs
Don't come back EU variants and
all

One potato, two potatoes, three potatoes four
Five potatoes, six potatoes, British potatoes for sure.

Cocka doodle doo my job is in the EU
My boss has lots of paperwork and doesn't know what to do.

Solitary solitary how does your UK grow?
 With silver bells and legal farewells
And new exports out on the go. Ho Ho

Boris put the kettle on

Boris put the kettle on

 Boris put the kettle on we'll all wait

and see

Govie take it off again Govie take it

off again, Govie take it off again

 EU membership's gone away

Diddle diddle dumpling my son

John

Was gridlocked and couldn't move

on

One step off and one step on

Stuck in a lorry my son John

Ring a ring of customs

A pocket full of sticking points

Gunships, Gunships

You all fall down

Three gunboats not nice

Three gunboats not nice

See how they run

See how they run

They all run after the EU sea life

Who cut off their quota with a

carving knife

Did you ever see such a thing in

your life as

Three gunboats not nice

The north wind doth blow and we
shall have snow
 And what will poor Brexit do then
poor thing
He'll keep in the warm but not
cause us much harm
And boost the economy in the
spring good thing

Interest rates are falling down
Falling down falling down
Interest rates are falling down
 Soon it's over maybe

Wee Willie lorries run through the
town
upstreets and downstreets causing
lockdown
Shouting through their windows
causing great gridlock
Are you ready for the new
paperwork it's quite a stumbling
block

Oh dear what can the matter be?

Dear dear what can the matter be?

Oh dear what can the matter be?

 Brexit has started   this year

They promised to give us a new

bunch of measures

To ensure that we saw a glimpse of

some pleasures

But a virus arrived and gave us

more pressures

To tie up the end of next year

To give us British fish and say

goodbye

One two De Gaulle blocks EU

Three four Wilson's referendum opens the door

Five six Thatcher worried on euro state fix

Seven eight opt out of Euro rate

Nine ten UKIP election win

Eleven twelve vote to leave held

Thirteen fourteen withdrawal flaunting

Fifteen sixteen May resignation seen

Seventeen eighteen Boris wins election

Nineteen twenty withdrawal 2020

To see other publications below by the author visit **snappysnappybooks.com** or just search **Dr Mike Pearce Amazon books.**

Many of these books in these volumes are also published individually

SNAPPY SNAPPY COLLECTIONS:

Volume 1. BUSINESS AND SELF CONFIDENCE

How to be a Successful Business Weed
Clingers, Creepers and Scramblers
How to Deal with Life's Snakes and Ladders
Trust-Nothing but a Must
Know Your Students and Build Your Image
Hidden from the Heart but not Forgotten
More Pens for Pops
Charity Shops

Volume 2. IDENTITIES, HANG UPS AND CONCERNS

I Herring Gull
Pulvi Royal
I am Termite
Go Fat Go
Make up-Revealed
Fertility Stones and Chocolate Eggs
Captain Grottbuster versus the Grey World

The kittiwakes Warning
Wastefulness-Bone and Urine
Tails, Tales
A slice of Slang with a touch of Cockney and a drop
of Dorset
Mr Hamstrings Dinner

Volume 3. HORROR AND HISTORY

The Living Fossils
My Therizinosaurus
Human Termites eat London
Pigeons Splat London
Glass Anemones Tentacle-ize London
Beware of Cucumbers, Apples and Pigs
The Cornish Urchin
Baby Toes
Googolplex of Mice
Screaming Alley
The Night Mare
Queen Rat on Deadman's Island
Dead Donkey Lane
Old Mother Nature laughed and Laughed
The Plaster Room

Volume 4. RELIGION AND HOPEFULNESS

Pattern for Purpose God's and Man's designs
The Littlest Oyster
Tuppeny Hangover
In a Dark, Dark Corner was the Holy Ghost
The Little Shepherd Boy's Gift

Spider in the Tomb
The Sparrows' Last Soul
The Pawnbroker's Souls
The Red Church Doll
The Boy who found Christmas
The Eggstraordinary Easter Egg
Little Mary
Shepherd's Purse
Sitting next to Angels
The White Lily-St Mildred-Patron Saint of Thanet

Volume 5. TIDE AND TIME

The Shell Man
The Shell Lady
The Watcher on the Fal
The Rock Pool
A Call under the Sea
Pocket full of Starfish
The Scrofula Infirmary
Till my Lips were Salt as Brine
The Man with a Book on his Head
Coloured Bricks
The Girl Under the Paeony Tree
Nothing but Leaves
The China Blackbird
The Man who Collected Figures
The Rusty Gate
Time Runs Dry (a play set in a care home)

Volume 6. **FAIRY TALES AND POEMS**

The Nursery Rhyme Cat
 Cats at Christmas

The Tuppeny Bear
The Giant and the Giraffe Boy
The Giant's Toothpick
The White Cockerel
The Old Pot and the Golden Shoes
Ball Rooms
Exodus to a Leaf
The Forlorn Fruit Fly
Two Sleepy Boys
Mrs Light and Mr Dark
 I'm Just Going to the Bathroom
The Tulip Tree
The Man who always Sprinted
Bits and Bobs (Poems and short stories for children)

Volume 7. **A VARIETY OF WOMEN**

Photosynthetic Women
Absorbed by a Woman
The Slothful Wife
Betty's Barcodes
Valentines Cards
The Lady loves Red
The Woman who Smelled Books
Boy, Could She Smell!
The Lady who loved Hairspray

Volume 8. CHRISTMAS BOOKS

Impy Christmas
The Little Shepherd Boys Gift
The Boy who found Christmas
Oh, father Christmas what yer going to do?
Nothing but leaves
The Tuppeny hangover
The China Blackbird
The Tuppeny Bear
Cats at Christmas
I Hate Christmas

Volume 9. HIDDEN PERCEPTIONS

Silhouette on the pier
I'm not a dinosaur
Mr Mucus
The golden steps
Napoleonic Frankenstein

Volume 10. MANY CURIOUS STORIES

The house that cries
The paint brush
The man who collected smiles
Jack and the ivy
The stolen baby
The angels quest
The silly isles
Wilderness Way
I am shadow
The lift

Volume11. CHRISTMAS BOOKS 2

Christmas butterfly
The man in the library
City of laughter, city of tears
Blower Armageddon
Happy Christmas
Antman
A fairy journey
The top of the hill
The Christmas visitor
Ring up an angel
The Christmas raindrop

Volume 12.FAITH AND FAME

Fight for Faith (Gordon of Khartoum)
Angel 1818 (James Blundell)
The Saint who carried his head (St. Denis)

Volume 13. A CORNUCOPIA OF SHORT STORIES

The cursing stone
Punch and Judy (New version)
Touch of Kent dialect
One in 20 million
Be a used seed (Finding new horions)
'Open Arse' (The maligned Medlar)
Wings of colour
Elephant pin-cushion

Volume 14 PLANTASTIC

One in twenty million
Be a seed(Finding new horizons)
The open arse (A maligned medlar)

Nothing but leaves
Exodus to a leaf
The tulip tree
Photosynthetic women
Shepherd's purse
 The girl under the paeony tree
Jack and the ivy
Baby toes
Half a flower
How to be a successful business weed
Clingers creepers and scramblers

Volume 15 INSECTASiA
I am termite
Mother of hundreds
The living fossils
Human termites eat London
Brief encounters with insects
Spider in the tomb
The forlorn fruit fly
The Christmas butterfly
Towers of wax
Antman

Volume 16 TA TA TALES
Condiment kiss
Half a flower
Towers of wax
Gee haw whammydiddle
Peeping Tom
Flowers in the snow
One hundred
Life's escalators
Swallowed by a whale

OTHER STAND ALONE PUBLICATIONS at
snappysnappybooks.com
Red Fred Cell and Friends (Human Biology -
advanced level
Ronnie's Sermon Snippets
Viking Bay-Natural History (Broadstairs, Kent)
The World of Wax
God rest you Merry Scrooge
Napoleonic Frankenstein
Satan's stars
HOP to Heaven
The White Lily-St Mildred-Patron Saint of Thanet

ABOUT THE AUTHOR

Dr Mike Pearce is a scientist interested in behaviour. He also was a lecturer in human biology and health at a college in Canterbury, Kent

For more information go to snappysnappybooks.com